A Poem Here,
A Poem There

Sherry Deines

BookLeaf
Publishing

Presentation by *BookLeaf Publishing*

Web: www.bookleafpub.com

E-mail: info@bookleafpub.com

ISBN: 9789357690409

First edition 2022

Dedicated to our beloved Miley. You will always be in our hearts.

ACKNOWLEDGEMENT

I would like to thank my family for their patience while I created the poems for my book. Thank you to my readers. I hope you enjoy reading my poems as much as I enjoyed writing them.

PREFACE

My dream since I was young was to write a
book.
I am so happy to have this opportunity to create
a book of poems.
I am hoping it will be enjoyed by many.
I also hope it will encourage others to chase their
dreams.

Cats

They are furry and funny
But cost lots of money.

They can be quiet and shy
But can also be very sly.

Their claws can be sharp
They could use them to play the harp.

You can sweep every day
But their fur still flies every which way.

They will steal your heart
But they are sneaky and smart.

Their tails are long
But closed in a door, things will go wrong.

You can give them a treat,
Five minutes later, they will want a repeat.

A pat on his head
Or some belly rubs instead.

Bring out the cat stroller
One will quickly run over.

A drink from the tap
Or scritches on his back.

Yarn

Yarn is fun, yarn is grand
I love to make things when I have it in my hand.

I love all the colors, every single one
When I decide on a color, that starts the fun!

So many choices of different kinds
Deciding on just one puts me in a bind.

What will I make and what will I do?
When it's all done, who will I give it to?

It may take me awhile to complete
But the finished creation can't be beat.

I soar through the pattern with the help of a cat
Because there's always a paw to give the yarn a
playful smack.

I'm done! This time around, the knots were few
I can gift it to someone and start anew.

Walking

One foot in front of the other, one step at a time
Do it this way and you will be fine.

Go out in the sun or even the rain, it doesn't
matter which
One you will stay dry and the other you will
itch.

Make sure your shoes are tied or your velcro is
done up
Because if you don't, you could end up with a
bump.

Don't look at your phone or read a book
Pay attention to the sidewalk and always be sure
to look.

If you see one of your neighbors, be sure to
wave
Because if you don't, the future could be grave.

Pet the neighbor's dogs as you walk by
Also be sure to tell their owners hi.

When you return from your long walk outside

I hope you are filled with a happy pride.

Chocolate

6

Creamy goodness
Hand it over now!
Often melts in the sun
Crazy if I don't get enough
Only the best for me
Lava cake is very good
Awesome for a snack
Tends to melt in your mouth
Easily eat every day

Leaves

Colorful and brittle
Plentiful and crisp
An explosion of colors
Make a fort with them before you rake them
Hide, run or throw them
Ride your bike through them
Peel the wet ones off your shoes
Walk on the sidewalk that's covered in orange,
yellow and red bursts of color.

Bees

Bees fly through the air
They soar looking for flowers
One is quickly found

Snails

A snail here, a snail there
Snails, snails everywhere.

Sometimes little, sometimes big
You may just find one on a twig.

Whether it's raining or whether it's sunny
You will find them to be kind of funny.

If you lose sight of one at the time
You can always find it by its slime.

They can be on the ground or way up high
There is no stopping them, but you can try.

Whether just one or a whole bunch
Take the time to watch them munch.

Hummingbirds

High in the sky
Unique
Marvelously fast
Made for flying
Incredibly cute
Near the flowers
Great at feeding from a feeder
Breathtaking
Itty bitty
Reach tall trees
Dainty
Sharp beak

Family

Love
Support
Encourange
Helpful
Guidance
Always there
A shoulder to cry on
Have your back
Reliable
Sympathetic
Advocate

Grandparents

12

Great at teaching
Really something special
Always positive
Never negative
Delicious desserts
Patient when you misbehave
Amazing at everything
Reasonable all the time
Elegantly dressed
Never doubted me
Taught me to knit and crochet
Showed me to to drive a tractor

Music

I listen to music when I am in the car
Especially if I need to go far.

I wish I could sing but I can't carry a tune
But maybe no one would hear me if I was on the
moon.

So music it is, one song at a time
I prefer the 80's which makes my family whine.

I'm careful not to have it too loud
Because that could make people nearby frown

Do you like music? If so, which kind?
Where do you listen? At home or on a beach in
the sand?

Everyone should listen to music at least once a
day
Little kids can listen as they play.

Ode to snow

Oh snow,
So very cold
White like a cloud
So fluffy as you fall from the sky

Oh snow,
You are silent
Big flakes land on the ground without a peep
Throw a snowball at a friend and you will hear a
thump and an ow.

Oh snow,
I feel cold if you soak my mitts
My nose will turn red because of your coldness
My feet could freeze in my boots.

Oh snow,
I remember making snow cream-Yummy!

Oh snow,
Without you, I would have never went sledding
growing up.

Fun on the Farm

I remember when I was young and I had so
much fun on the farm.
I'd go see my Grandparents every summer.
There was a huge mud puddle that I would sit in
with my cousin.
I had a lot of fun with my cousins who were
younger than me.
We would make bale houses which was fun but
itchy.
There was a horse to ride and lots of cows to
watch.
I remember the plastic wading pool we would
swim in.
The horse flies would fly and makes us go
under the water.
My Grandparents had an attic that had a lot of
fun stuff to look at.
I remember the big trucks full of grain.
They had the biggest garden in the backyard.
There was no running water and we had to use
the outhouse to go to the bathroom.
I remember that outhouse getting knocked over
by a bull chasing Unlce Willie.
I remember that outhouse getting knocked over
by a bull chasing Uncle Willie.

Just once...
'Cuz I almost drove it in the ditch.
Showed me how to drive a tractor

Feral Cats

When we lived in Fremont, there were feral cats
everywhere
It made us sad because we care.

They came in all colors: white, beige, striped
and black
There were so many, it was hard to keep track.

Every day we'd go out with a big container of
food
We wanted to give some to all and not be rude.

We loved them all and we were sad when we
moved
We were sure they were possibly confused.

But we found great folks to take over for us
Everyone was so helpful, it was a plus.

We hope they are well, every furry one
And enjoy their days in the warm California sun

Friends

They are important to have
They will always have your back
They are there for the good times and for the bad
They won't ever let you down
They will always laugh at your jokes
They will listen to you whine about everything
They will help you if you are in a bind
They are good to watch a movie with or go eat
some dinner
Everyone needs friends.

Christmas

Cool gifts for all
HO HO HO
Really cold outside
Icicles on the trees
Santa Clause
Tinsel on the tree
Miniature lights
An assortment of cookies
Small elves getting into mischief

Rain

I don't like rain during the day
It interferes when you want to go outside and
play.

Your feet get wet unless you have on boots
So if you have to choose a pair, make sure they
are cute.

Your clothes will get wet and stick to your skin
Better get home and put on dry ones with a grin.

You may need an umbrella to help keep you dry
It'll keep the raindrops off your head as they fall
from the sky.

It's fun to throw rocks into a big puddle
As you and your friends stand together in a
huddle.

Find a curb with water flowing down
Make a paper boat and watch it float around.

Put your bathing suit on and run around like
crazy
Then after the rain stops you can go to the pool
and be lazy.

If you live where it is dry, you will need lots of
rain
But if you live where it is wet, too much rain
will be a pain.

Pumpkins

Pumpkins are for fall
In October carve them all
Or make pumpkin pie

Bun Bun

Bun Bun stayed with us
We were happy to have him
He now has a home

Flowers

24

Full of color
Lovely
Only last a short time
While at our house
Easy on the eyes
Really nice smell
Send someone flowers today

Mother

My best friend
One on one time together
Takes time to listen
Happy times together
Excellent cook
Really cool